"An abundance of modern discourse characterizes persons as being a spirit that *has* a body. More accurately, we are an integrated body-soul unity. Our bodies matter. Further, writes Paul in his letter to the Corinthian Church, our bodies are 'temples' of the Holy Spirit. In *Restoring Your Temple*, Dr. David Hager outlines pathways to achieve holistic body-spirit restoration. Through practical guidance drawn from biblical wisdom, readers are encouraged to honor God and experience wholeness by transforming their bodies into healthy and holy temples."

—KEVIN BROWN

President, Asbury University

"Dr. W. David Hager is a powerful writer of truths that the Apostle Paul used to compare our physical bodies to the temple of the Holy Spirit! He is giving a blueprint for an abundant life! Dr. Hager is releasing scientific facts and profound reflections that challenge us to be all God designed us to be in his kingdom! This is a must-read book!"

—COY BARKER

Orator and author

"Dr. David Hager offers scriptural insights and practical wisdom for restoring those areas of our lives damaged by sin. Your journey toward healing can start today."

—GREG SMALLEY

Vice president, Marriage and Family Formation, Focus on the Family

"A doctor's expertise is human biology. Being a psychiatrist, I love when physicians use their critical thinking, people-centered gifts to dig past the physical sphere, thus examining the more profound aspect of our design, our PsychoSpiritual Sphere. Dr Hager compassionately pulls the curtain back on this sphere in Chapter 8, 'Do a Thorough Honest Inventory', which specifically and practically unpacks, I believe, the most crucial step catalyzing transformation. Even though Apostle Paul walked thru the other steps, he was still stuck on the Romans 7 hamster wheel. A deeper inventory process opens the door to reveal the destructive files of misinformation (columns 3–5) stored in our unconscious mind. Now we are equipped to destroy strongholds by actually taking every thought (not just our conscious ones) captive to the obedience of Christ resulting in true joy, peace, and freedom. "

—KARL BENZIO

MD, board certified psychiatrist, Honey Lake Clinic

Restoring Your Temple

Other Books by W. David Hager, M.D.

The Real Truth About Sexually Transmitted Diseases

The Reproduction Revolution (ed)

Infection Protocols for Obstetrics and Gynecology (ed)

Stress and the Woman's Body

As Jesus Cared for Women

On the Way; Ministering in the Moment

*Simmering Anger, Smoldering Rage; The Emotions
That Are Tearing Our World Apart*

Restoring Your Temple

Seven Steps to Inner Healing and Peace

W. DAVID HAGER

Foreword by ED TRAUT

RESOURCE *Publications* · Eugene, Oregon

RESTORING YOUR TEMPLE
Seven Steps to Inner Healing and Peace

Resource Publications
An Imprint of Wipf and Stock Publishers
199 W. 8th Ave., Suite 3
Eugene, OR 97401

www.wipfandstock.com

PAPERBACK ISBN: 979-8-3852-3394-6
HARDCOVER ISBN: 979-8-3852-3395-3
EBOOK ISBN: 979-8-3852-3396-0

Scripture Quotations

Tag Lines

Your individual temple can be damaged as much by disuse as by external forces.

Hezekiah's 7 steps of restoration align perfectly with our modern steps for recovery.

The purpose of temple restoration is to create a place where Holy Spirit can dwell.

Often it isn't the felonies of life that desecrate our personal temples, but rather the misdemeanors.

Don't focus as much on the *what* of your life as on the *why*.

Our personal temple can be desecrated by making poor life choices even after making an initial good choice.

Restoration based on a personal relationship with the Passover lamb results in healing and peace.

The debris that contaminates your personal temple, your body, must be removed, destroyed, then replaced with a renewed mind and heart.

Restoration is a journey toward wholeness which will not be completed until we see Jesus face to face.

Table of Contents

Foreword

Ed Traut

WHEN WE STUDY THE Bible, there is often a tendency to interpret the Old Testament as, well old; and the New Testament as newer or more modern as it relates to our life's circumstances. However, it is important to understand that God's Word is true and can be trusted because there are applications from both the Old and the New to our lives today, and the attributes of Jehovah, God are revealed accurately in both.

Throughout my life, many concepts have attempted to influence the quality of my living including academic teaching, presentations, books, media and even physicians. Exercise, eat well, get more sleep, take this prescription, read this, do that, have been recommended to benefit my lifestyle. However, in this significant contribution to the literature about recovery, a more lasting and important lifestyle is revealed directly from the Word of God to enable one to acquire lasting inner healing and peace.

In *Restoring Your Temple*, Dr. W. David Hager has taken an Old Testament excerpt; correlated it allegorically with a New Testament teaching of the apostle Paul; and detailed for us how those guidelines for life can be applied to the ministry of personal recovery which we all desperately need.

The ancient Hebrew temple was a focal point of Jewish life where persons came to worship God, seek his forgiveness and praise him for all of his mighty acts toward his people. The historic temple of God is regarded as the holiest place on earth for any

Jew. Paul, as a Jew himself, recognized this and used the allegory
of God's Spirit being able to reside within us as a temple which
should be kept clean and wholesome in order for God to dwell in
it.

Even today, in Israel, there is a deep longing and working to-
wards restoring the temple for God's people which was always the
important symbol and indictor of His relationship and dwelling
with mankind.

Hager found specific steps outlined by King Hezekiah in II
Chronicles for restoration of the ancient temple which had been
damaged by disuse and disrepair. Hager is the first to recognize
that the steps detailed by Hezekiah of moving out of denial of sin
and addiction; recognizing we are powerless to change on our own;
seeking the help of others to aid us in our recovery process; doing
a thorough inventory of our lives indicating whom has hurt us and
whom we have hurt; and finding that a personal relationship with
Jesus Christ as the higher power in our lives are the only ways to
find true, lasting inner healing and peace. He then correlates those
steps with modern steps for recovery and restoration of our spiritual, emotional and relational lives when they have fallen into sin
and various addictive behaviors. As with all Biblical teaching, he
then encourages us to teach these steps of restoration to others as
we are taught in Deut 11:18–19

> *Fix these words of mine in your hearts and minds; tie them
> as symbols on your hands and bind them on your fore-
> heads. Teach them to your children, talking about them
> when you sit at home and when you walk along the road,
> when you lie down and when you get up.* NIV

This is emphasized again by Paul in his letter to Timothy.
II Tim 2:2

> *For you must teach others those things you and many oth-
> ers have heard me speak about. Teach these great truths to
> trustworthy men who will, in turn, pass them on to others.*
> TLB

This divine revelation to Dr. Hager of these spiritual guidelines can be life- changing if we are willing to read and apply them to our own lives which often have some element of dysfunctional behavior. His lengthy work in the field of recovery ministry, where he has seen many lives restored to freedom from the chains that bound them, adds credence to its content.

I find his teaching to be of critical importance today as we find in ministry, so many persons struggling with problems associated with substance use and abuse, sexual dysfunction, marital disharmony, gambling, dishonesty in business, anger, rage, lack of respect for the sanctity of human life, co-dependence and many other addictive behaviors. I strongly urge you to read this timely and powerful book, and apply the steps to your own life which may be in need of restoration in one or more areas. Then make note of the steps of recovery and go back to them whenever you begin to feel that your personal temple is falling back into disuse or disrepair. I believe this book about inner restoration is a "must read" for believers and non-believers. Our thanks to Dr. Hager for digging out these pearls of wisdom from the old and bringing them into today! My prayer is that you will find the inner healing and peace that God promises those who put their faith in Him.

Preface

ARE YOU DEALING WITH issues which seem to have taken control of your life? Has your internal compass turned from true North. Have you tried to regain stability with religion, church, small groups, even counseling, to no avail? In *Restoring Your Temple*, you will be guided through the most frequent hurts, habits and hangups which can result in disuse and disrepair of your individual temple, and be directed to specific steps to use as tools in repairing the damage that has been done. Incorporating the seven steps of recovery on a daily basis will enable you to find the inner healing and peace you long for. As the apostle Paul said, you will be able to glorify God in your body.

When we hear the words church, synagogue, cathedral, or temple we generally think of a place where believers of a particular faith go to express their worship and praise to the god they believe in and trust. In the days of the Old Testament, according to the Hebrew writings, the Israelites belief was that God resided in a structure known as a temple. The people came to worship and praise Jehovah there; to offer gifts of thanksgiving; to seek forgiveness of their transgressions; and to ask for blessing and favor. In essence, God was housed in a tent or building and in order to worship him one was required to come to his house.

However, when we read the New Testament, we are introduced to a new concept of the temple. Certainly, believers were not discouraged from attending the temple to share in their praise and worship of God with other followers; but they were given a new definition of where God resides. Instead of being spatially- limited by the walls of a structure, we are told by Jesus himself and then by the apostle Paul, that God can and will reside within us. Instead of us seeking his residence; he seeks us by sending his only Son to give his life for the forgiveness of our sins, and promises the gift of Holy Spirit to guide and direct our lives. Thus, we become personal-temples where God can reside and indwell with his Spirit. John 15:15–17

> *"If you love me, obey me; and I will ask the Father and he will give you another Comforter, and he will never leave you. He is the Holy Spirit, the spirit who leads into all truth. The world at large cannot receive him, for it isn't looking for him and doesn't recognize him. But you do, for he lives with you now and someday shall be in you."* TLB

In I Cor 6:19–20, Paul extends this concept of Holy Spirit residing in believers by relating our bodies to sites where God's Spirit can dwell.

> *Do you not know that your bodies are temples of the Holy Spirit, who is in you, whom you have received from God? You are not your own; you were bought at a price. Therefore, honor God with your bodies.* NIV

For this third person of the Trinity to come and inhabit our lives we must first, by faith, accept Jesus as Savior and Lord of our life and receive the grace (receiving what we don't deserve) God offers to those who confess this belief.

> John 3:16, *For God so loved the world that he gave his one and only Son, that whoever believes in him shall not perish but have eternal life.* NIV

> Rom 10:9, *If you declare with your mouth, "Jesus is Lord," and believe in your heart that God raised him from the dead, you will be saved.* NIV

> John 14:6, *Jesus answered, "I am the way and the truth and the life. No one comes to the Father except through me.* NIV

Eph 2;8-9, *For it is by grace you have been saved, through faith—and this is not from yourselves, it is the gift of God—not by works, so that no one can boast.* NIV

The apostle Paul taught us that we receive the gift of the presence of Holy Spirit in our lives when we accept Jesus as Savior and Lord. Some believe this happens at the moment of conversion, while others believe there is a "second work of grace" or sanctification process which must occur separately. I am not here to argue that because it is not critical to our discussion of restoration. I am saying the indwelling presence of Holy Spirit in our lives is crucial to living out our faith on a daily basis. He enables us to live spiritually healthy lives. Rom 8:9–10, NIV

> *You, however, are not in the realm of the flesh but are in the realm of the Spirit, if indeed the Spirit of God lives in you. And if anyone does not have the Spirit of Christ, they do not belong to Christ. But if Christ is in you, then even though your body is subject to death because of sin, the Spirit gives life because of righteousness.*

So, if God offers Holy Spirit to reside in those who believe in Jesus as his Son and as the Savior of the world, it becomes imperative that we keep the temple of our body spiritually clean and healthy since he doesn't desire to reside in a dwelling that is contaminated by sin and in disrepair from lack of use.

This doesn't mean when we mess up, God leaves us and rejects us. On the contrary, we have the promise of his willingness to forgive and forget every sin if we confess it and repent. Repentance meaning turning in a new direction away from the sinful behavior.

> I John 1:9, *If we confess our sins, he is faithful and just and will forgive us our sins and purify us from all unrighteousness.* NIV

> Isa 43:25, *"I, even I, am he who blots out your transgressions, for my own sake, and remembers them no more.* NIV

In *Restoring Your Temple*, we will discuss the various forms of the temple built for God's residence from the Old Testament narrative; the revolutionary concept of God's Spirit residing within our human bodies; how our individual temples can fall into disuse or be contaminated by sin and/or addictive behaviors; and what steps can be taken to restore the temple (body) back to functional use as an instrument of God's kingdom. We will also talk about how we can maintain restoration of our personal temples and reach out to others with the message of restorative hope for them.

In my years of leading recovery groups, I frequently encounter persons who have difficulty believing the creator and sustainer of the universe could and would actually dwell within them. Years of sin and addiction resulted in feelings of inadequacy and a certainty they could never measure up to a standard that would be deserving of a holy God wanting to empower them with his Spirit, much less supernaturally live within them. Convincing them that Rom 8:1 is true is often very difficult.

One day as I was preparing a recovery lesson, I came upon II Chron chapters 28–30. Ahaz, king of Judah had closed the doors of the temple in Jerusalem that Solomon had built. After his death, his son, Hezekiah became king and realized the temple of God had come into disuse and disrepair. I recognized seven distinct steps Hezekiah laid out for repairing the temple, and the instructions he gave the priests to carry out so it would be restored to functionality. Now those steps were intended to restore the Jewish temple of ancient days, but I found that the very same steps could allegorically be applied to the restoration and recovery of our minds and bodies when they become contaminated with sin and addiction. As I described those steps to persons in our groups, they were often able to recognize the corollary between their lives being individual temples and the need to have those temples restored in a stepwise fashion. They were frequently empowered to incorporate them into their daily living and see dramatic transformation in their lives; moving from a dependence upon self and others to life-changing dependence upon a God of restoration and renewal.

The seven steps outlined by Hezekiah are very similar to the twelve steps used in many recovery programs, but they are distinct and direct in their purpose. In order to encourage you on your journey to wholeness, I have incorporated stories of individuals who have successfully worked these seven steps into their lives and had their individual temples transformed and restored.

I fully recognize the Old Testament writings were applicable to what was occurring in that day and time, but I also believe that word was God-directed in the same way the New Testament writings were in proclaiming the New Covenant. Paul used the structural temple as an example of a place where God could reside and receive the praise of his people, and correlated it with his Spirit dwelling within our physical bodies. He knew the Jewish people would hopefully understand the allegory. Centuries later, we need to take a new look at this profound word of hope and transformation.

Perhaps you are thinking, I don't live a life of addictive behavior, but we all have covert or overt sins in our lives which may prevent God's presence from being fully manifest in our personal-temples because of misuse or damage inflicted by ourselves or others. *Often it isn't the felonies of life that desecrate our temples, but rather the misdemeanors.* No matter where you are spiritually, we can all use a fresh look at restoration. This book describes the steps necessary to clean up our house and make it presentable for God's spirit to inhabit.

> Rom 3:23, *For all have sinned and fall short of the glory of God.* TLB

Am I saying that Holy Spirit absolutely cannot dwell in us unless we are totally cleaned up inside? No, it is not impossible, and perhaps not improbable, but according to the Word it is unlikely he can continue to dwell in an individual temple that continues to be contaminated by sin and addiction because both are contrary to his nature and existence.

So many persons live in denial of the hurts, habits and hangups in their lives and never do the deep, bucket-work necessary to recognize the root issues or why they act out in the manner they do. We learn to deny unacceptable behaviors at a young age in order to escape punishment. Thus, habits of lying, denying and blaming others become our modus into later years of life.

This book is intended to benefit persons from teen years to older ages. It will help you to recognize dysfunctional behaviors; the causes of those actions; and the steps to take to resolve them and find lasting restoration in your life.

It is my prayer that application of these steps of restoration in your life will help to bring about the same type of transformation that people in our groups have experienced; whether it be from sin or any type of addictive behavior you may have had in the past, or are dealing with in the present. Holy Spirit desires to inhabit your temple, but you have to make the choice to ask Jesus in, welcome his presence and then follow his guidance and direction as to how you need to open wide the doors of your temple and submit to the restorative work he desires to do. If you do, I am confident that you will find a pathway to inner healing, peace and renewed life. Prov 21:21

> *Whoever pursues righteousness and love finds life, prosperity and honor.* NIV

Let's walk through this step-by-step process together. Be patient because the steps are in order for a reason and need to be processed one by one. If you get hung-up on a step you should always go back to Step one and re-initiate the process. I assure you if the process of restoration is led by Holy Spirit, it can be trusted and applied because it works, resulting in right living (righteousness).

CHAPTER 1

The Old Testament Temple

In order to understand Paul's description of the body as a temple of God's Spirit to the Corinthians, we need to realize how the Jewish temple came about.

When the Israelites fled Egypt after 430 years of slavery, God guided them to a miraculous crossing of the Red Sea and into the wilderness beyond. He promised to guide them with a pillar of cloud by day and a pillar of fire by night.

Moses led the people of Israel into the desert. God called Moses and seventy-three others to come up onto Mt. Sinai. Then Moses was instructed to come to the very top of the mountain where he stayed for forty days and nights and was given the stone tablets with the ten commandments of God inscribed upon them. God gave Moses specific instructions about making a tabernacle in which the people would worship and praise Jehovah himself, as described in Ex 25:8–9.

> "Then have them make a sanctuary for me, and I will dwell among them. Make this tabernacle and all its furnishings exactly like the pattern I will show you. NIV

This tabernacle was to be a place for God's glory to dwell and a place of worship, remembrance, confession and commitment. Within the tabernacle were the ark of the covenant with an atonement cover containing the commandments of God; a table with the bread of the presence on it; a lampstand; and the altar of burnt offering. The outer Holy Place was separated from the inner Most Holy Place by a curtain. The ark of the covenant with the atonement cover was placed in the Most Holy Place.

Moses also often took a tent and pitched it outside the camp of the Israelites which he called the tent of meeting. He would go there to inquire of God and to receive instructions about how to lead the people. God's glory would appear around the tent when he spoke to Moses, and when Moses exited the tent, his face was radiant with that glory[1]

This was the beginning of the tabernacle or temple of God with the children of Israel. However, it would be years until an actual temple was constructed.[2] King David's son, Solomon described this in II Chron 6:4-11.

> Then he said: "Praise be to the Lord, the God of Israel, who with his hands has fulfilled what he promised with his mouth to my father David. For he said, 'Since the day I brought my people out of Egypt, I have not chosen a city in any tribe of Israel to have a temple built so that my Name might be there, nor have I chosen anyone to be ruler over my people Israel. But now I have chosen Jerusalem for my Name to be there, and I have chosen David to rule my people, Israel.' "My father David had it in his heart to build a temple for the Name of the Lord, the God of Israel. But the Lord said to my father David, 'You did well to have it in your heart to build a temple for my Name. Nevertheless, you are not the one to build the temple, but your son, your own flesh and blood—he is the one who will build the temple for my Name.' The Lord has kept the promise he made. I have succeeded David my father and now I sit on the throne of Israel, just as the Lord promised, and I have built the temple for the Name of the Lord, the God of Israel. There I have placed the ark, in which is the covenant of the Lord that he made with the people of Israel." NIV

1. Purkiser WT (ed), Exploring the Old Testament, Beacon Hill Press, Kansas City, MO. pp 125-27.

2. Ibid, p202

Later, the nation would be divided into a northern kingdom (Israel) and a southern kingdom (Judah). Israel attacked Judah and damaged the temple built by Solomon in Jerusalem. When Joash became king of Judah, he ordered the temple to be restored to its original specifications. However, Jehoash would later lead Israel against Judah and ordered a portion of the Jerusalem wall to be destroyed and articles to be taken from the temple. The people of Judah vacillated in their devotion to proper worship of God in the temple and it actually came into disuse and further disrepair under the leadership of king Ahaz.

Ahaz's son, Hezekiah became king when he was twenty-five years old. He attempted to follow God's direction in leading the people. Hezekiah became aware the temple was in disrepair and ordered the priests to initiate its restoration. He directed them to follow seven essential steps of renovation which I will describe in the section on restoration of the temple.

The people of Judah would return to the rebellious ways of pagan, idol worship. As a result, God allowed the Babylonians (modern day Iraq) to attack Jerusalem and destroy its walls, city gate, buildings and temple. The people were carried into captivity in Babylon for seventy years. The Persian empire (modern day Iran) would overwhelm Babylon and under the leadership of Cyrus and Darius allowed the Jews to return to their homeland and initiate the rebuilding of the gates and walls under the direction of Nehemiah and the temple under the leadership of Ezra.[3]

These events lead us to the temple that Paul was referring to when he spoke to the Corinthians about the body being a temple where Holy Spirit could dwell. He recognized God could not be contained within a structure. God's presence was everywhere. He had sent his Son to be born of a virgin, live among us, be crucified, buried and raised from the dead by this Holy Spirit who Jesus promised could and would live in us to guide and direct our paths as believers.

---

3. Purkiser WT, (ed) Exploring the Old Testament, Beacon Hill Press, Kansas City, MO. pp 389–90

Paul's understanding was not shared by all of those to whom he was speaking. He desired to create an allegory of a structure, the temple, which they could readily identify with, and the New Covenant description of their minds and hearts being a spiritual residence in which Holy Spirit could dwell in an intimate and individual way. Paul emphasized how important it was to keep their personal temples clean and hospitable so God's Spirit could have a receptive place to inhabit.

This was a difficult concept for the Jewish people to grasp. How could the God of the universe, whom they had been taught resided in a building, actually want to leave that place and live inside of them? Paul wanted them to understand that it had always been God's design to set up tabernacle within them individually so they could experience him in a personal relationship of love, devotion and commitment.

Hezekiah gave us a description of how such a temple should be restored, but first we must review how our own individual temples can be damaged and fall into disrepair from without and from within. Perhaps you are thinking, "I don't have any major sins or addictions in my life; I don't need guidelines for restoring my body spiritually, physically, emotionally or relationally." Remember my statement, it isn't the felonies of life that desecrate our personal temples, but rather the misdemeanors. It isn't murder, rape, adultery, robbery, assault, etc. we are talking about here. It is the misdemeanors of lust, gossip, slander, cheating, uncontrolled social drinking, misuse of prescription medications, habitual lying, gambling, use of pornography, etc. which end up causing disrepair of our minds and bodies that Paul was referring to in the I Corinthians passage. Thus, we all need to look carefully within to see if application of the steps may enhance our daily living.

CHAPTER 2

The Allegory of God's Temple in Us

ALLOW ME TO GO a bit deeper into the reasons why Paul painstakingly emphasized the concept of a personal temple before we get into Hezekiah's 7 steps of restoration. Although it may seem redundant, it is essential to your understanding of God's plan for your personal healing and redemption.

When he made the allegorical comparison between the ancient temple in Jerusalem and the human body, he was doing just that; creating an allegory. Paul understood the Jewish people recognized the temple as a site where God's presence dwelled and could be tangibly felt. For centuries, those who believed in Jehovah God, went to the temple to worship and to have sacrifices offered to atone for their sins and shortcomings. The Spirit and glory of God was felt to reside there. This was a place where persons could humbly beseech God to forgive them and restore them to right living.

Paul's teaching emphasized Jesus' promise to his followers (John 14:17) that after his death and resurrection, Holy Spirit would be sent by God to not just reside in the world, but to actually live as spirit within each believer-- to lead, encourage and comfort them. Paul was and is teaching us that you don't have to go to a structure to find God's Spirit; he desires to reside within you so that you become an individual-temple in which he, as the third part of the Trinity, can live.

In our recovery ministry work, I have found this to be a difficult concept for those who have been living in sin and addiction to accept. "How can God's Spirit live in me?" they ask. Frequently I hear, "There is nothing good in me; I can never measure up to what God and others want me to be; I've tried over and over before and always end up defeated. How can I maintain a lifestyle that will qualify me as a temple, a residence for God? And even if that is possible, how do I maintain my temple so his Spirit doesn't reject me and leave like all the other people I have ever trusted and believed in during my time on earth?"

Jesus taught us that Holy Spirit is sent to come alongside us as a teacher, guide, leader, and even a comforter. God knows we need a helper along our way, and he willingly provides that assistance with his presence. He doesn't expect us to be able to do the work of restoration on our own; so, in a supernatural way he has arranged for his Spirit, the Holy Spirit to reside in us. He isn't here to condemn us for who we are or were, but to enable us to be the very person God created us to be. Rom 8:1

> *Therefore, there is now no condemnation for those who are in Christ Jesus.* NIV

In Acts 2, Peter told the people if they believe, and repent of their sins, God would fill them with the presence of Holy Spirit. Peter, like Paul, was emphasizing if God's Spirit could in the past, reside in a structure we call a temple; he is now offered to you to live within you as personal temples for his dwelling.

Paul's point is, if he can reside in us, we need to keep the place of his residence clean and free from sin and addiction to the best of our ability; understanding that according to I John 1:9, if we do sin, we can confess, repent and be assured of God's forgiveness.

As I mentioned, it was at this point in my study of Holy Spirit supernaturally indwelling our bodies that I came across Hezekiah's steps for cleaning up and restoring the temple. Those steps jumped off the page at me, as being very similar to what is required to restore our lives to God's care and control when we have or are living in a way that isn't pleasing to him.

If you are like me, you often want to get to the main point of emphasis without identifying and understanding the events that led up to that part. It is like the person who is dealing with dysfunctional behaviors in their life and want them to go away without coming to grips with the *root issues* that cause their acting out in the first place. So, before we list the seven steps which are essential for the clean up and repair of our individual temples, we must review how they came into disuse and dysfunction in the first place. I'm sure Hezekiah would have wanted to wave a magic wand over the temple and see it restored to its original form, but *pixie dust* restoration isn't effective or lasting. We will spend some time reviewing dysfunctional behaviors, and their root causes. So, please don't jump ahead to the seven steps of restoration yet, there is a method to the madness!

CHAPTER 3

Causes of Temple Destruction

WHEN WE READ THE Old Testament description of the temple, our focus is often drawn to its ultimate destruction by enemies of Israel who invaded the land. However, when Hezekiah became king at twenty-five years of age, he discovered [as recorded in II Chron 29] that the temple had been desecrated and was in disrepair. It wasn't from external sources; rather it was from internal disuse and idol worship that had become prevalent among the people. That is one reason Paul used the ancient temple as an allegory for new believers to understand their bodies were temples and should be valued as such. He also emphasized that our individual temple could not only be damaged and destroyed by external sources, but often by the internal damage we inflict upon ourselves which is a result of not taking care of our minds and bodies properly.

External effects such as disease, accidents, poor nutrition, lack of adequate sanitation, etc. are still very prevalent in the world and can harm or even destroy our temple. It is the internal things, however, that can do as much harm to our bodies and minds. Paul took his teaching about our bodies being temples directly from a lesson of Jesus found in Mark 7:20–23 describing such internal effects.

> He went on: "What comes out of a person is what defiles
> them. For it is from within, out of a person's heart, that
> evil thoughts come—sexual immorality, theft, murder,

adultery, greed, malice, deceit, lewdness, envy, slander, arrogance and folly. All these evils come from inside and defile a person." NIV

Both Jesus and Paul were referring to how sin and addictive behaviors can contaminate, and defile our mind, heart and spirit to the extent that the damage is the same or worse than if our temple is attacked and destroyed by an invading army.

If we desire God's Spirit to live in us; to guide and direct us; to lead us in right living (righteousness); we must keep the place where he dwells hospitable, clean and in good repair. Making personal choices to overeat, overdrink, take prescription medications in unhealthy ways, use substances, not maintain good hygiene are recipes for disaster to our temple. Submitting to the temptation of sexual sin and addiction is always destructive to our body; realizing as Jesus taught, that such sin has its origin in our heart and mind before we ever act out. In addition, associating with persons who encourage us to engage in such activities, does nothing to enable us to move away from such behaviors. Self-control is listed last with the fruit of the Spirit, but it may be the most important attribute, along with love, for us to maintain.

I often teach that lust is our greatest addiction. Desiring things that do not belong to us, leads us to engage in activities to obtain those things no matter how unhealthy. I am not just talking about sexual lust. Lust for anything is not beneficial because it results in allowing our minds to be controlled and often manipulated by that desire, so we yearn to possess something or someone that isn't our's. Lust can cause us to feel we will not survive unless we have what our mind is set on. Alcohol, substances, overeating, acting out sexually, pornography, an unhealthy need to control others, can all fall under this umbrella of lust. These desires actually result in idolatry; putting little gods before the one, true God. The temptation may come from without, but the choice to submit comes from within.

Jesus recognized lust as a sin of the heart within our temple and addressed it in Matt 5:27–28.

"You have heard that it was said, 'You shall not commit adultery.' But I tell you that anyone who looks at a woman lustfully has already committed adultery with her in his heart." NIV

What one lusts for often gives them a dopamine-high in the brain; resulting in a desire to lust for more, get more, and make poor choices about how to achieve the thing desired, or possess the person desired.

Greed is equally damaging to our personal temple. We see, we want, and we develop plans for how to obtain material things that are above and beyond our real needs. The rich, young ruler came to Jesus asking what he needed to do to obtain eternal life. He indicated he had kept all of the commandments, but when Jesus recognized his deep-seated root issue of a desire for material things and asked him to go and sell what he had; give to the poor; and then come and follow him; he was unable to do so and went away sad. He allowed his temple to be destroyed by greed.

It isn't uncommon to feel we can engage in some dysfunctional behaviors as long as most of our living is acceptable. In counseling, I have found this to occur in the lives of believers who have rationalized that submitting to one temptation, such as pornography, is okay as long they don't act out in other ways. The problem is most sins and addictions don't occur in the singular. The young ruler had a root issue of greed, but also of a need to control. Jesus wanted the young man to come and follow him, but he couldn't because he wanted to maintain control of his life rather than submit to the leadership of another. Mary Magdalene had seven evil spirits. Legion had many addictions.

In Luke 8 we read the story of the man named Legion. He was called Legion or "Many" because he had numerous addictions or evil spirits tormenting him. He didn't have just one issue contaminating his temple. Several dysfunctional behaviors had invaded that space and driven him to engage in activities that frightened others and were destroying his life. He was basically isolated because harmful and addictive behaviors controlled his daily existence. Apparently, he recognized how damaged his temple was because as soon as Jesus got out of his boat and approached the shoreline; this man, who was destroyed from within, approached the Master and sought deliverance. It took a touch of Jesus to free him from his tormentors and restore his temple as a place where the Spirit could reside.

In the Old Testament, these behaviors were often referred to as idol worship. Today, we may be subtly led into a lifestyle of addiction to things that end up controlling our existence and causing harm and even destruction of our temple. I often hear phrases like, "Oh I just drink a little bit;" "I smoke pot, but it will never lead me into harder drugs;" "Sex outside of marriage actually makes our marriage better;" "As long as the bank will keep loaning it to me, I'll keep spending it;" "I only take pain medication when I am really hurting." We are willing to give up certain habits, but rebel when encouraged to lay every issue down at the foot of the Cross. Sin is sin, and addictions are addictions. Attempting to categorize them making one worse than another is a recipe for temple destruction.

The end result is internal destruction caused by external forces and substances. You feel that a bit of temporary satisfaction will not affect your journey toward permanent fulfillment. Don't deny me the opportunity to get high occasionally. Don't restrict my sexual indulgence as long as no one else knows about it. Don't prevent me from watching stimulating videos on line that excite me. Don't tell me that acting out in anger as a result of righteous indignation is wrong. Don't restrict my spending or tell me I can't gamble. Don't tell me not to gossip about or criticize others. Don't indicate that posting of harmful comments on line isn't my right to free speech. All of these activities slowly and progressively tear our temple apart and prevent us from being a viable residence in which God's Spirit can exist.

If Satan can get his foot in the door in one area, he will gradually attempt to convince you that other dysfunctional aspects of behavior aren't important either. God is a jealous God and desires your total devotion; the commitment of your individual temple to his care and control.

But what if you are engaged in one or more of these behaviors? Is there any hope for restoration and renovation of your personal temple? Absolutely! That is where Hezekiah's steps come into effect in order to allow you to find true healing and peace or as Paul would say to glorify God by the way you live.

I will expand on Hezekiah's seven steps to restoration of your personal temple in order:

Step 1- Open the Doors of Your Temple

Step2- Recognize You Are Powerless to Restore Yourself on Your Own

Step 3- Confess Every Sin and Addictive Behavior

Step 4- Turn Every Area of Your Life Over to God's Care and Control

Step 5- Do A Thorough, Honest Inventory

Step 6- Thank God for Your Restoration

Step 7- Accept Jesus, the Passover Lamb, as Your Savior

Take them one step at a time, and don't move on to the next step until you have completely dealt with the prior one. Let's get started.

CHAPTER 4

The First Step of Restoration: Open the Doors

ALTHOUGH KING HEZEKIAH OUTLINED the steps necessary for restoring the temple built by King Solomon in Jerusalem with the intention that a physical structure would be brought back to functional use; I have found that those very same steps can be applied to our physical bodies and minds when we have allowed ourselves to fall into sins and addictive behaviors that result in destruction from within as well as without. In the next seven chapters, I will review those steps individually and discuss how their application can result in restoration of our individual temples so we can find inner healing and lasting peace.

The steps must be worked in order and we cannot skip a step and still be successful in navigating the process to complete restoration. In II Chron 29:1–3, the first step of moving out of denial that there was any damage to the temple is described.

> *Hezekiah was twenty-five years old when he became king, and he reigned in Jerusalem twenty-nine years. His mother's name was Abijah daughter of Zechariah. He did what was right in the eyes of the Lord, just as his father David had done. In the first month of the first year of his reign, he opened the doors of the temple of the Lord and repaired them. NIV*

When one has incorporated sin and/or addictive behavior into the fabric of their life, it can easily become so habitual that the dysfunction isn't recognized as being abnormal or wrong and is denied for what it really is. Thus, the first step is to move out of denial into total, honest confession of every habit or hang-up that has contaminated our inner being. This requires opening the doors into our self-life; admitting every dysfunction and confessing them openly to God and to someone we trust. The emphasis in the previous sentence is on *every*. Failing to admit every sin or addictive behavior will ultimately result in relapse back into one or more of those dysfunctional acts.

Denial is defined as a false system of beliefs not based on reality. It is refusing to admit the truth or reality about someone or something. It is a trait that all persons who are living in sin or addiction have along with lying, shaming and blaming.

Before we can admit our tendency to addictive behavior to God and to someone we trust, we must admit to ourselves that we have issues and behaviors that require resolution in order for us to be healthy, functional individuals. If we deny dysfunctional behavior to ourselves, we will never admit it to God much less to someone we trust.

Because the people had denied their need of God for such a long time, the temple had fallen into disrepair and the doors shut so no one could enter, confess their sin, and experience forgiveness and healing. We can do the same thing in our lives. Subtly, we begin to act out in order to satisfy our desire for temporary satisfaction; and before we know it a habit or addiction results. Remember, addiction is not just about drugs, alcohol and sex. Many dysfunctional behaviors can become addictive. Some of those may even be considered functional by today's values.

When confronted about the problem, we often deny the act(s) itself or fail to admit it is harming us in destructive ways. The behavior becomes a part of what our personal temple is and we begin to confuse the dysfunction with who we really are. Over time we fear if we give up this habit or hang-up, we will not experience any satisfaction or enjoyment in life. This is what we call seeking *temporary satisfaction* rather than finding *permanent fulfillment*.

We learn to deny at a young age in order to escape punishment. When confronted about doing something wrong, the first words out of our mouth are, "No, I didn't do that." Denial becomes a habit and soon we use it to avoid punishment or identification for wrong-doing of any sort. The doors to our real self are shut to the outside world and can prevent anyone from gaining entrance to help us improve or clean up our individual temple.

We often live in denial with God also. We come to believe he isn't aware of our secret sins and addictions, when in fact, he knows everything we are involved in. So, we must admit these things to ourselves and to him in order to achieve a restored temple. Phil 3:7-9

> *The very credentials these people are waving around us as something special, I'm tearing up and throwing out with the trash—along with everything else I used to take credit for. And why? Because of Christ. Yes, all the things I once thought were so important are gone from my life. Compared to the high privilege of knowing Christ Jesus as my Master, firsthand, everything I once thought I had going for me is insignificant—dog dung. I've dumped it all in the trash so I could embrace Christ and be embraced by him. I didn't want some petty, inferior brand of righteousness that comes from keeping a list of rules when I could get the robust kind that comes from trusting Christ—God's righteousness.* Msg

As Hezekiah instructed, we must take the first step by opening the doors of our life, admitting our need for help and restoration, and allowing the clean-up process to begin. The first step is often the most difficult because we have become comfortable living in our dysfunctional world of sin and addiction. Many of the people around us have also become comfortable with us in a dysfunctional state and prefer that we remain in such a condition rather than change.

It often takes a crisis or significant pain as a stimulus for opening up and crying out for help. Hezekiah's father, Ahaz had resorted to the worship of many, little gods instead of the one, true God. In our recovery ministry, I refer to these little gods as the idols of addictive and dysfunctional behavior. It wasn't until Hezekiah recognized this idol worship and resolved to correct it by opening the doors of the temple and allowing restoration to occur that real healing began for the people.

Another reason we persist in our denial of dysfunctional behavior is we honestly believe if we admit who we really are, no one will love us, respect us or want to associate with us. Since others won't forgive us, we have difficulty forgiving ourselves. We incorrectly conclude that the things we have done are so bad there is no way God could ever forgive and restore us. The Bible is full of examples of just such persons who were forgiven, delivered and restored; and in Isaiah 43:25 we are told that God is not only willing to forgive, but also to forget our shortcomings.

King David was a murderer and adulterer. Mary Magdalene was a prostitute. The woman at the well had a sexual addiction. Zacchaeus was a thief. The apostle Paul persecuted and killed believers. Peter denied that he knew Jesus. Yet, each of these persons was forgiven and restored when they admitted their sin and addictions and opened the doors of their lives to the life-changing power of Jesus.

What are some of the behaviors you may be in denial about? An unhealthy use of pain medication or sedatives. A dependence on alcohol or drugs. A habit of lying to distort the truth and escape punishment. Jealousy of what others have. An inability to control a need to gamble. Use of pornography, suggestive material, or on-line sexual encounters. Lust for power and control of others. Allowing the behavior of others to determine how you feel about yourself; which is co-dependency. Stealing or shop-lifting. Non-marital sex. Underlying anger. [see *Simmering Anger, Smoldering Rage; The Emotions That Are Tearing Our World Apart*, Wipf and Stock]

If a behavior is one you would not want others to know about, and don't feel God would approve of; I would encourage you to admit it; seek God's forgiveness; open the doors of your personal temple to his restorative power; repent by moving in a new direction and begin to live a restored life daily in peace with yourself, others and God himself.

> Isa 43:25 *I, even I, am he who blots out your transgressions, for my own sake, and remembers your sins no more.* NIV

> I John 1:9 *If we confess our sins, he is faithful and just and will forgive us our sins and purify us from all unrighteousness.* NIV

> Rom 8:1 *So, there is now no condemnation awaiting those who belong to Christ Jesus.* TLB

In II Chron 29:7 we are told the temple was so closed up that even the porch doors were sealed; the external lights put out; the inner flame of the temple extinguished; and no offerings or worship of God occurred. Hezekiah's Step 2 describes how we are powerless on our own to bring restoration to such a dark place in our individual temples.

CHAPTER 5

The Second Step of Restoration: Powerless on Your Own

I AM CERTAIN MOST of you are familiar with the 12 Step programs that have been used to change the lives of millions of persons addicted to alcohol, drugs, sex, etc. The original program, Alcoholics Anonymous, was designed by Bill Wilson and that format has been adapted to conform to the other areas of addictive behavior. In order to bring a recovery program into the Christian arena, John Baker developed a Christ-centered, 12 Step, 8 Principle program and named it Celebrate Recovery. Christ-centered because the *Higher Power* who can enable the addict to enter into sobriety is not an ambiguous source, but is specifically named Jesus Christ.

We have established that the Apostle Paul referred to our bodies as temples where Holy Spirit can dwell. So, the temple where the Israelites believed Jehovah resided in a structure built by man; becomes a human temple, created in the likeness of God, where he can exist as the third part of the Trinity. As such, he can live in and through us and enable us to live according to his design and plan as Christ-followers.

If our body becomes addicted to acts or substances that harm our temple, it falls into disrepair and the Spirit of God cannot dwell in a place where sin is in residence. It is our responsibility to keep the temple clean and to make choices that honor the structure and don't contaminate it.

I have used the Celebrate Recovery curriculum to lead groups for the past 30 years and have seen hundreds of lives transformed, relationships restored, families rejoined, and persons surrender their lives to Christ. So, I wasn't shocked but I must admit a bit surprised when I found that King Hezekiah had outlined 7 steps for temple restoration which correlate intimately with the previously mentioned programs. What did he know about recovery over twenty-five hundred years ago? He recognized steps were required in order to evaluate damage and facilitate restoration of a facility called a temple which Paul allegorically related to our minds, hearts, spirits or in total, our bodies.

In chapter 4, I discussed the first step which must occur-moving out of denial that one has a problem, into admission a change is needed in order for restoration to begin. The first step is to admit the *temple* is in disrepair and requires a significant change in order to be made hospitable again as described in II Chron 29:3.

> In the very first month of the first year of his reign, he re-opened the doors of the Temple and repaired them. TLB

Hezekiah indicated the doors of the temple had been shut tight preventing people from being able to seek God, worship him, confess their sins and make offerings to him. As a result of this disuse, the temple was filthy and contaminated by debris. Thus, he ordered the hinges to be repaired and the doors opened. He moved out of denial that there was a problem and admitted change must begin within before it could be recognized from without. Then he moved rapidly on to Step 2. II Chron 29:4

> He summoned the priests and Levites to meet him at the open space east of the Temple and addressed them thus: TLB

In his wisdom, he recognized repair of the temple could not occur in his own strength. He realized he was powerless to take on such a task alone and called on others to assist him in this endeavor. Obviously, he also recognized he would need God's help if this restorative process was to be successful. So, Step 2 is as critical as Step 1; once you move out of denial into admission of a hurt, habit or hang-up, you must seek the help of God and of others in order to achieve full restoration of your personal temple.

When we live with sin in our lives, it is not uncommon to believe we can stop this behavior whenever we desire. The pride we harbor allows us to rely on self to resolve our issues with no need to turn to others including God for assistance. Apparently, the children of Israel had become content with their temple being in disrepair and felt no need to seek assistance in restoring it. They went about their daily activities with the doors to the temple closed up tight. They made no attempt to gain access and begin the process of recovery from their dysfunctional behavior. It often takes others to make us aware of our deficiencies and shortcomings so healing can begin. In this case it was Hezekiah who alerted the people to come to the realization of the need for temple reconstruction.

We must recognize our human limitations and stop trying to resolve our issues on our own. First, we must seek God's help in opening the doors of our life to his care and control and then seek the help of programs and individuals to help us begin the cleanup process. David recognized this helplessness in his own life as stated in Psalm 51:1–4

> *Have mercy on me, O God, according to your unfailing love; according to your great compassion blot out my transgressions. Wash away all my iniquity and cleanse me from my sin. For I know my transgressions, and my sin is always before me. Against you, you only, have I sinned and done what is evil in your sight; so you are right in your verdict and justified when you judge.* NIV

Then we must reach out to others for guidance and fellowship in order to maintain a restored state. When we are living in sin and addiction, we are living to please our self-life which is called our *flesh*. If one leaves off the last letter of the word and reverses the spelling of flesh, the word is *self*. Living in the power of self has resulted in the dysfunctional lifestyle we exhibit. Life becomes unmanageable and out of control. Sound familiar?

Admitting your powerlessness to save and restore yourself is not a sign of weakness, as others might have you believe; but rather a sign of inner strength that you have the courage and insight to recognize you need God's help and the assistance of others to overcome the obstacles in your life and move into healing and recovery.

Jesus addressed the issue of being powerless on our own in John 15:5.

> "Yes, I am the Vine; you are the branches. Whoever lives in me and I in him shall produce a large crop of fruit. For apart from me you can't do a thing." TLB

When you recognize you are powerless on your own to clean up the mess within and seek the help of others through a recovery program, I encourage you to find a Christ-centered program with a record of low recidivism. When you attempt to find others to assist you in your restoration, please locate persons who have dealt with your sin/addiction otherwise you will not receive the particular help you need. If you have experienced rejection, abandonment, abuse, neglect, parent-wounds; find individuals who can identify with your hurts so they can advise you how to overcome those root issues. Don't seek out persons who are not living in recovery and who are still dabbling in their habits. You need help to stay on the road, not advice that will result in your taking detours along the way. You know the path to dysfunction and don't need anyone to lead you back down that road. You will have to make changes in whom you associate with and where you have gone to achieve temporary satisfaction.

I realize you may have been lied to and misled by persons in the past, which prevents you from trusting any individual or any program to help you recover without condemning you or judging you. I assure you from my own experience and from the stories of many others, the first step in recognizing you are powerless on your own is to seek God's help for he can be trusted. As noted in Heb 10:23

*Now we can look forward to the salvation God has prom-
ised us. There is no longer any room for doubt, and we can
tell others that salvation is ours, for there is no question
that he will do what he says.* TLB

Then, find trustworthy, committed individuals who are devoted to helping you restore your personal temple with sound
advice and a solid example lived out daily. Hezekiah sought out
priests and Levites, but there are many persons who are not in the
ordained ministry who can offer reliable help in cleaning up and
restoring your temple because they have been there and done that.

It is time to stop denying your pain and face it; to stop playing God and lay down *self*. You must admit your powerlessness to
save yourself on your own and seek God's guidance and plan for
restoration and redemption. If you truly submit to his will and his
ways, you will be empowered to overcome every obstacle that has
inhibited restoration in your life. Isaiah 40:29–31

*He gives strength to the weary and increases the power of
the weak. Even youths grow tired and weary, and young
men stumble and fall; but those who hope in the Lord will
renew their strength. They will soar on wings like eagles;
they will run and not grow weary; they will walk and not
faint.* NIV

Then you will be ready to move to step 3 and continue the clean-up
process.

CHAPTER 6

The Third Step of Restoration: Confess Everything

HEZEKIAH RECOGNIZED THAT THE act of opening the doors of the temple and acknowledging he was powerless on his own to restore it wasn't enough. A step of intervention was required. The filth and debris accumulated over the period of disuse had to be thoroughly cleaned out. II Chron 29:5–6

> *He summoned the priests and Levites to meet him at the open space east of the Temple and addressed them thus: "Listen to me, you Levites. Sanctify the Temple of the Lord God of your ancestors—clean all the debris from the holy place. For our fathers have committed a deep sin before the Lord our God; they abandoned the Lord and his Temple and turned their backs on it.* TLB

God said much the same to Ezekiel in Ezek 11:18

> *And when you return, you will remove every trace of all this idol worship.* TLB

Over time, sin and addictive behaviors can become such a part of the fabric of our lives that they go unnoticed and are no longer seen as wrong. Lying, cheating, stealing, lusting, coveting, jealousy, greediness, the desire to control others can subtly creep into our daily lives and actually become idols to us. We act spiritual in church and appear upstanding in our community and around some of our acquaintances, yet there is a pile of debris within our hearts and minds that contaminates our individual temple. The longer it goes unchecked, the higher our trash heap becomes.

Jesus' story of the Lost Sons in Luke 15 is not only to tell us about who Daddy is really like, and to reveal how he waited patiently for the rebellious son to realize he was lost and needed to repent and return home; but is a revelation of how lost we can be while believing we are doing everything right. The elder son had allowed self-sufficiency, works and unforgiveness to become such a part of his life he was unable to rejoice when his younger brother came to his senses and returned home. He had lived for so long with bitterness and resentment in his heart, he had no idea how lost he was. He needed a thorough restoration and was totally unaware of it. Even when Daddy himself came out to reason with him and invite him into the celebration, he was unable to admit he was as lost as his younger brother who had rebelled and wandered off.

Hezekiah didn't tell the priests and Levites to clean out enough of the trash so people could again return to the Temple; rather he instructed them to clean out *all of the debris* which had built up over time. There was so much garbage there the people could not begin to present themselves to God in an environment which would facilitate seeking his mercy and grace.

The same is true for us today. You can't confess some of your sins and admit some of your addictions expecting restoration of your individual temple. It requires a thorough, total, complete confession of every sin, habit, and yes, every hurt to clean up your heart, mind and spirit. Holding back on confession of even one dysfunctional behavior will cause regret down the road. Holy Spirit wants a clean temple in which to dwell. This doesn't mean you have to be perfect; it means you must be willing to allow him to clean you up by forgiving your sins and addictions so you are presentable for his presence. I John 1:9 assures us of this.

> But if we confess our sins to him, he can be depended on to forgive us and to cleanse us from every wrong. And it is perfectly proper for God to do this for us because Christ died to wash away our sins. TLB

Jesus understood this need for a thorough housecleaning when he was quoted in Matt 12:43–45

> "When an impure spirit comes out of a person, it goes through arid places seeking rest and does not find it. Then it says, 'I will return to the house I left.' When it arrives, it finds the house unoccupied, swept clean and put in order. Then it goes and takes with it seven other spirits more wicked than itself, and they go in and live there. And the final condition of that person is worse than the first . . ." NIV

In *On the Way; Ministering in the Moment*, I describe a pastor (name and address changed) who came to our recovery program seeking healing from his sexual addiction. Over several sessions, he confessed to me his unfaithfulness to his wife and addiction to pornography. He wanted it all to just go away with that confession, but was unwilling to confess his acting out to his wife or congregation. As it turned out he also had an addiction to gambling. It wasn't until three years later, after struggling with guilt and shame, he was able to thoroughly confess every hurt, habit and hang-up which he dealt with, and find true healing with restoration of his marriage and his ministry.

In my early conversation with this pastor, I had reminded him of another man with many addictions named Legion who was described in Mark 5:1–20.

> When they arrived at the other side of the lake, a demon-possessed man ran out from a graveyard, just as Jesus was climbing from the boat. This man lived among the gravestones and had such strength that whenever he was put into handcuffs and shackles—as he often was—he snapped the handcuffs from his wrists and smashed the shackles and walked away. No one was strong enough to control him. All day long and through the night he would wander among the tombs and in the wild hills screaming and cutting himself with sharp pieces of stone. When Jesus was still far out on the water, the man had seen him and had run to meet him, and fell down before him. Then Jesus spoke to the demon within the man, and said, "Come out, you evil spirit." It gave a terrible scream, shrieking, "What are you

going to do to me, Jesus, Son of the Most High God? For God's sake, don't torture me!" "What is your name?" Jesus asked, and the demon replied, "Legion, for there are many of us here within this man." Then the demons begged him again and again not to send them to some distant land. Now as it happened there was a huge herd of hogs rooting around on the hill above the lake. "Send us into those hogs," the demons begged. And Jesus gave them permission. Then the evil spirits came out of the man and entered the hogs, and the entire herd plunged down the steep hillside into the lake and drowned. The herdsmen fled to the nearby towns and countryside, spreading the news as they ran. Everyone rushed out to see for themselves. And a large crowd soon gathered where Jesus was; but as they saw the man sitting there, fully clothed and perfectly sane, they were frightened. Those who saw what happened were telling everyone about it, and the crowd began pleading with Jesus to go away and leave them alone! So, he got back into the boat. The man who had been possessed by the demons begged Jesus to let him go along. But Jesus said no. "Go home to your friends," he told him, "and tell them what wonderful things God has done for you; and how merciful he has been." So, the man started off to visit the Ten Towns of that region and began to tell everyone about the great things Jesus had done for him; and they were awestruck by his story. TLB

Total, honest confession of every sin and addiction is essential to achieve healing and restoration. When this occurs, God can and will deliver us from every hurt, habit and hang-up and send us out, as he did my pastor friend, to tell others the good news of our temple restoration.

Partial confession leads to partial repentance and ultimately to dabbling in sin and addictive behaviors. Hezekiah understood the process so that no dirt, no filth would be left in the Temple to ultimately contaminate the house of God. We are no different. In order for our bodies to be temples where Holy Spirit can dwell, we must voluntarily get rid of everything that prevents a deep housecleaning. This doesn't mean we will never sin or fall short again, rather it allows us to live in the knowledge we are not condemned by a failure if we confess it and repent of it.

When thorough, honest confession occurs there is a sense of peace and freedom that will wash over you and truly restore you. It is also beneficial to find someone you trust implicitly to confess your actions to. When you confess to such a person the thoroughness of your admission takes on a reality that may be missed in confessing to God whom you cannot see. Finding you are not shamed, blamed or condemned is a life-changing experience that continues the restoration of your personal temple and prepares you for the next step of turning your life and will over to God's care and control.

CHAPTER 7

The Fourth Step of Restoration: Turn Every Area of Your Life Over to God's Care and Control

ONCE YOU HAVE MOVED out of denial that you have a need for restoration; recognize your powerlessness to save and restore yourself; and confess every sin and addictive behavior; it is time to turn every area of your life over to God's care and control. Hezekiah recognized there needed to be a thorough removal of everything that kept the temple from complete restoration and that involved cleaning up every room no matter how long it took. II Chron 29:15–17

> *They in turn summoned their fellow Levites and sanctified themselves, and began to clean up and sanctify the Temple, as the king (who was speaking for the Lord) had commanded them. The priests cleaned up the inner room of the Temple and brought out into the court all the filth and decay they found there. The Levites then carted it out to Kidron Brook. This all began on the first day of April, and by the eighth day they had reached the outer court, which took eight days to clean up, so the entire job was completed in sixteen days.* TLB

It requires courage to begin the process of restoration; teamwork to carry it out; and persistence to see it to completion. It is in doing things our way and seeking our own will, shutting out God and the influence of others that gets us into a place of dysfunctional living and contamination of our individual temple. We come to believe we don't need a higher power, Jesus, to enable us to live a life of stability and sobriety from our substances of choice. A voice within tells us, "You can do this on your own. You don't need anyone else to help you or guide you. You're in control, you call the shots, you deserve self-satisfaction." That is the evil one attempting to convince you there is no need to turn your life and will over to anyone else; you are good on your own.

Turning your life over to Jesus is a decision he will never go back on. As he said from the cross, "It is finished." You don't have to recommit your life to him every time you mess up and fall short of his desire and plan. You recognize your failure, confess it to him and repent by turning in a different direction; away from acting out in a similar way.

Turning your will over to his care and control requires a daily commitment to Bible reading, prayer and meditation. His will is for you to have a restored and renewed temple where his Spirit can dwell daily. He doesn't want the door of your life to be shut. He doesn't want you to live in denial of overt or covert sin and addiction. He wants to guide you into a life of peace and contentment so your personal temple can be a testimony of his restorative power. By submitting your will to him, you will find a path of escape from every temptation to sin and act out as recorded in I Cor 10:13.

> *No temptation has overtaken you except what is common to mankind. And God is faithful; he will not let you be tempted beyond what you can bear. But when you are tempted, he will also provide a way out so that you can endure it.* NIV

It would seem Hezekiah recognized a belief in God wasn't enough to keep the temple clean. A definite submission of his own will and the will of the people to follow God's direction in the process of restoration was key to definitive transformation and to maintaining a restored temple. He called the priests and Levites to help him. We need to have sponsors and accountability partners to keep us on track and help us complete the daily bucket work required to pursue our restoration. Attempting to do this on our own often leads to frustration and failure. Two or three are better than one. Eccl 4:12.

> *And one standing alone can be attacked and defeated, but two can stand back-to-back and conquer; three is even better, for a triple-braided cord is not easily broken.* TLB

When our mind and heart are committed to following our own will, we find ourselves doing the same things over and over again, expecting a different result each time, and that is the definition of insanity. What is required is a mind renewed by the Spirit. Rom 12:2.

> *Do not conform to the pattern of this world, but be transformed by the renewing of your mind. Then you will be able to test and approve what God's will is—his good, pleasing and perfect will.* NIV

The influences of the world want you to believe transformation isn't necessary. They tell you everything is okay as it is. Enjoy life; do whatever you desire; don't submit to any guidelines, especially spiritual ones; and for certain don't allow anyone to think you are in need of a Higher Power. I can assure you those influences do not bring you lasting restoration and contentment. Turning every area of your life over to his care and control is the pathway to inner healing and peace.

With life and will submitted to him we can then begin doing a thorough inventory of our individual temple as Hezekiah described in step 5.

CHAPTER 8

The Fifth Step of Restoration:
Do a Thorough, Honest Inventory

KING HEZEKIAH DEMANDED THE priests and Levites do a thorough inventory of the clean-up process including every article which was removed and those which were cleaned and restored. He understood a complete inventory was essential to documenting and stabilizing the recovery process as recorded in II Chron 29:18–19.

> *Then they went back to the palace and reported to King Hezekiah, "We have completed the cleansing of the Temple and of the altar of burnt offerings and of its accessories, also the table of the Bread of Presence and its equipment. What's more, we have recovered and sanctified all the utensils thrown away by King Ahaz when he closed the Temple. They are beside the altar of the Lord."* TLB

When a company conducts an inventory, it compiles a complete list of all of its goods in stock as well as all possessions necessary for conducting business. It is a necessary process for ensuring every article is accounted for and is in good repair. Damaged goods can be discarded and every item restored to its proper place in the building.

In order to solidify your recovery and restoration it is important to take the step of doing a moral and spiritual inventory. This is not a process to undertake until you are living in recovery and have the courage to address every hurt, habit and hang-up in your life. You must not only identify every person or thing that has hurt you, but also whom you have harmed. It must begin from the earliest events right up to the present and then should be continued frequently when you are living out your restored life. It involves evaluating relationships with others, priorities in life and attitudes of behavior.

Hezekiah didn't order the inventory to be done as his first step. Rather, he waited until the restoration process was nearing completion. My advice to you is do not initiate your inventory until you are stable, have others around you who can help you with this process and are willing to address every issue thoroughly and honestly.

When you embark on your inventory, I would suggest creating a notebook or journal with columns. In the first column you will list every person or thing that has harmed you relationally, emotionally or physically. You must go all the way back into your childhood and identify each one. It may be a person, but also could be an event or group who initiated the damage which resulted in your fear, anxiety, resentment, etc. Then you will need to list every person you have harmed in similar ways. As with each of these categories, don't rush through the process and be as thorough and honest as you possibly can. Often identifying one person or thing which harmed you will bring to mind others who have done the same. As uncomfortable as this process may be, it will result in significant emotional healing as your personal temple is restored.

Once you have listed the earliest encounter you can recall which had a negative effect upon your life, you will carry that line across the page to complete four additional columns. So, the columns from left to right will be the person or thing, the cause, the effect, the damage, and my part.

The second column is the Cause. In this section list what specifically the person or thing did to you to cause pain, anger, rage, resentment, isolation, etc. Do not hold back in identifying exactly what was done to you, or what you did to someone else.

Remember to be thorough and brutally honest. Be prepared for feelings of anger, disgust, resentment and even depression as you move through this column, but stay focused on the long-term healing you will experience.

Column three is the Effect. What was the acute effect of the act perpetrated upon you or that you inflicted upon someone else. Attempt to recall exactly how it made you feel in the moment of the act and what your immediate reaction was. This can often be an extremely emotional time in the process. After all, you are listing people and things that harmed you in perhaps devastating ways. Be specific and don't hold back in the false assumption you can soften the blow. Hezekiah told the priests and Levites to list every single item without hesitation. This is the only way to accomplish complete restoration.

Column four is the Damage. You have identified the acute effects of the harm done to you and that you did to others; now is the time to list the chronic effects those actions have had on your life. How have they affected you emotionally, relationally, physically, spiritually; not just in the moment, but later in life. Perhaps you isolated yourself; experienced overwhelming resentment; became fearful of things or persons who would not ordinarily cause fear; felt you could never measure up, developed phobias, etc. Once again, being thorough and totally honest is key to working through to restoration of your personal temple.

Column five is Your Part. In this column you will list your response and reaction to each of the hurts inflicted upon you. This is your personal response to each and every specific event that has resulted in dysfunctional living. Did you respond with anger and rage? [In *Simmering Anger, Smoldering Rage; The Emotions That Are Tearing Our World Apart* I discuss how to identify and deal with your emotions of anger and rage.] Did you attempt to exact revenge upon the person? Have you maintained an attitude of unforgiveness and resentment that plagues you to the present? Have you made amends to a person whom you harmed? What was your role in the dysfunctional process listed in the Cause?

Please remember if you were a victim of abuse or neglect by the person listed in column one, your part is to be listed as *none*. You were not the cause of the action, but were a victim of it. It may have been impossible for you to forgive your perpetrator, but remember until you are able to at least be willing to do so, that person, unfortunately, maintains some control over your life. I often suggest writing out a note of forgiveness, reading it to someone you trust, and then burning the note when you are unable to do this in person. I have even had persons whose perpetrator is deceased, write out a note of forgiveness, take it to the grave site and read it there.

Jesus considered offering forgiveness and making amends to be a critical part of your journey with God. Matt 5:23–24,

> *"Therefore, if you are offering your gift at the altar and there remember that your brother or sister has something against you, leave your gift there in front of the altar. First go and be reconciled to them; then come and offer your gift.* NIV

In this inventory process there are three aspects to forgiving others and making amends to those you have harmed. First, you need to accept God's forgiveness of your sins and addictive behaviors. Perhaps you feel your actions were so horrible they can never be forgiven. Maybe, because of poor child-rearing, you feel you can never measure up to standards set for you. Possibly you have bought into a works theology and think you have to do enough to merit God's forgiveness and favor. After opening the doors of your personal temple; moving out of denial you have issues; and confessing the sins and addictive behaviors which beset you; you can trust God's promise to forgive and forget. I John 1:9,

> *But if we confess our sins to him, he can be depended on to forgive us and to cleanse us from every wrong.* TLB

Isaiah 43:25

> *I, even I, am he who blots out your transgressions, for my own sake, and remembers your sins no more.* NIV

Second, you need to offer forgiveness to those who have hurt you and make amends to those you have harmed. Letting go of the anger and releasing it through forgiveness is the only way to find freedom from the acts perpetrated upon you and find true peace in your spirit. This is never easy but is always rewarding. As Jesus said in Matt 6:14–15,

> For if you forgive other people when they sin against you, your heavenly Father will also forgive you. But if you do not forgive others their sins, your Father will not forgive your sins. NIV

How often do we have to forgive others? Jesus basically said, "Don't put a number on it." Matt 18:21–22,

> Then Peter came to him and asked, "Sir, how often should I forgive a brother who sins against me? Seven times?" "No," Jesus replied, "seventy times seven." TLB

Thirdly, you need to forgive yourself. This is often the most difficult aspect of the process. We hang on to our sins and addictive behaviors even after we have asked God to forgive us. He promises to do it, but we don't allow his forgiveness to penetrate our minds. He has the capacity to supernaturally forget our sins, but we don't have that capacity and relive them over and over in our minds. It is time to forgive yourself and to believe Rom 8:1,

> Therefore, there is now no condemnation for those who are in Christ Jesus. NIV

After you have completed the initial inventory process (this may require many sheets of paper), I strongly encourage you to read it to your sponsor, accountability partner or someone else you trust implicitly. This brings a sense of finality to this initial process. However, your inventory is never totally complete. I recommend that you learn to journal in an inventory process. In this way, you can list the person, cause, effect, damage and your part for events as they occur in your restored life. You will learn to manage the section, *your part*, more effectively with each passing event!

Once you have completed your inventory, you will feel a sense of emotional exhaustion but then excitement and joy. Thus, you will be led into a desire to complete Step 6, praising and honoring God for the progress you are making in the restoration process.

CHAPTER 9

The Sixth Step of Restoration: Praise God for Restoring You

HOPEFULLY YOU HAVE MOVED out of denial that your temple was damaged; admitted every sin and addiction that has or is plaguing your life; recognized you are powerless to save and restore yourself on your own; repented of these acts which means you have turned to walk in a new direction away from every hurt, habit and hang-up; turned every emotional, relational and spiritual area of your life over to God's care and control; and initiated the process of doing a thorough, honest inventory of every act perpetrated upon you or which you have done to others. Now you are ready to thank God for initiating the process of restoration so his Spirit can dwell within your restored personal temple and enable you to walk in healing and peace daily.

Hezekiah recognized the source of temple restoration and instructed the people to praise and worship God for enabling them to accomplish this process. He wanted them to understand who was the benefactor of their cleaning out and cleaning up work. II Chron 29:25–30.

> *He organized Levites at the Temple into an orchestral group, using cymbals, psalteries, and harps. This was in accordance with the directions of David and the prophets Gad and Nathan, who had received their instructions from the Lord. The priests formed a trumpet corps. Then*

Hezekiah ordered the burnt offering to be placed upon the altar, and as the sacrifice began, the instruments of music began to play the songs of the Lord, accompanied by the trumpets. Throughout the entire ceremony everyone worshiped the Lord as the singers sang and the trumpets blew. Afterwards, the king and his aides bowed low before the Lord in worship. Then King Hezekiah ordered the Levites to sing before the Lord some of the psalms of David and of the prophet Asaph, which they gladly did, and bowed their heads and worshiped. TLB

Initially, when you move from sin and addictive behaviors into forgiveness and recovery there are constant reminders it was the grace of God that enabled you to be restored. However, as time passes, we sometimes tend to forget to thank and praise him for his mighty right hand that reached down to lift us out of the pit of turmoil and despair and set our feet back on solid ground. The sixth step instructs us to honor him for the reclamation work he has carried out in us. A part of our daily time alone with him should be to say, "Thank you, Abba, for all you have done to restore my life and give me inner peace and contentment. I owe you praise for revealing my hidden sins. I know this could never have occurred had you not intervened in my inner life."

We refer to Psalm 107 as the *addict's psalm*. It describes homelessness, hunger, depression, anxiety, being enchained to addictive behaviors, rebellion, physical disease, unmet expectations and even relapse. However, at the end of each stanza the psalmist indicates the people cried out to the Lord in their trouble and he delivered them from their distress by breaking the chains that bound them and cutting through the bars that held them captive. Then the psalmist goes on to write in verses 8, 15, 21 and 31.

Let them give thanks to the Lord for his unfailing love and his wonderful deeds for mankind. NIV

It is important to pause and identify the specific areas of turmoil and disrepair in your life and recall how God has stepped in to bring healing and restoration. For some of you this process may have been sudden, almost instantaneous; but for most recovery is a slow, steady transformation, and you must learn to trust the process. You have admitted you were powerless to save yourself on your own and were in desperate need of a higher power to step in and reconstruct your life. So, take time daily to thank him for his unfailing love, mercy and grace extended to you and for helping you clean up your personal temple so his Spirit can live in and through you!

There should be an emphasis on daily time alone with God. I encourage you to find a Bible translation that speaks to you personally. I often use my phone app which contains several translations so I can compare the content. I recommend reading a Psalm, a Proverb, as well as an Old Testament passage and a New Testament passage daily. It is often beneficial to have a Bible commentary or a devotional guide to which you can refer. In addition, I find journaling to be a great way to record the impact of God's word to me and to monitor my progress spiritually, emotionally and relationally.

I also encourage you to think of and thank others who have played a role in this redemptive process. None of us can do this alone. The relationships we establish on our way to recovery are invaluable and lasting. Remaining in a body of believers who accept you and pour into you is key to maintaining restoration. This may be a church group; a recovery program; or a small body of persons committed to being set free from sin and addictive behaviors. I believe, as Hezekiah directed, the pathway to achieving lasting healing, inner peace and complete restoration is through a personal relationship with Jesus Christ!

Having this attitude of gratitude brings us to the seventh of Hezekiah's steps of restoration. Accepting the Passover lamb (Jesus) as the perfect sacrifice for all of our confessed sins and addictions.

CHAPTER 10

Step 7: Receiving Jesus as Your Redemption

HEZEKIAH WASN'T AWARE HE was leaving us steps for recovery when he detailed the guidelines for temple restoration, but he couldn't have finished the work any better than to describe the one, true higher power who could redeem us from sin and addictive behaviors into a life of healing, peace and contentment. Now, I realize some of you may feel this step is out of order. Shouldn't receiving Jesus have been the first step? I believe Hezekiah recognized until the mind, heart and spirit of the person's temple is cleared of the debris which has interfered with the ability to worship God as he deserves; the individual cannot truly accept the Passover lamb and his work of redemption on the Cross. Thus, he introduces Jesus as the final step in complete restoration of our temple. This is described in II Chron 30: 13–15 and 18b-20.

> And so it was that a very large crowd assembled at Jerusalem in the month of May for the Passover celebration. They set to work and destroyed the heathen altars in Jerusalem, and knocked down all the incense altars, and threw them into the Kidron Brook. On the first day of May the people killed their Passover lambs. Then the priests and Levites became ashamed of themselves for not taking a more active part, so they sanctified themselves and brought burnt offerings into the Temple . . . since many of the people . . . were

47

ceremonially impure because they had not undergone the purification rites, the Levites killed their Passover lambs for them, to sanctify them. Then King Hezekiah prayed for them, and they were permitted to eat the Passover anyway, even though this was contrary to God's rules. But Hezekiah said, "May the good Lord pardon everyone who determines to follow the Lord God of his fathers, even through he is not properly sanctified for the ceremony." And the Lord listened to Hezekiah's prayer and did not destroy them. TLB

This order of steps isn't really any different than Jesus own plan for his devoted followers. He called his twelve disciples to follow him and learn from him before they ever truly believed he was the Messiah and the one who could forgive their sins and restore their lives. They were asked to commit and belong before they believed and as a result they obtained the inner healing and peace the seven steps offer, culminating in a personal relationship with Jesus.

The sacrifice of the Passover lamb had to be repeated over and over for the forgiveness of the sins and addictive acts of the people, but Jesus as the sacrificial Passover lamb gave his life once and for all so we could be forgiven, cleansed and restored to right standing with God. Thus, this seventh step is the crucial one for solidifying the movement from sin to forgiveness, from addiction to sobriety, from rebellion to redemption, from death to life. A personal relationship with Jesus is the key to inner healing and peace which lasts. This is described in the following passages:

John 14:6- *Jesus answered, "I am the way and the truth and the life. No one comes to the Father except through me."* NIV

Rom 10:9- *If you declare with your mouth, "Jesus is Lord," and believe in your heart that God raised him from the dead, you will be saved.* NIV

Acts 2:38–39- *Peter replied, "Repent and be baptized, every one of you, in the name of Jesus Christ for the forgiveness of your sins. And you will receive the gift of the Holy Spirit. The promise is for you and your children and for all who are far off—for all whom the Lord our God will call."* NIV

Heb 10:12–14- *Every priest goes to work at the altar each day, offers the same old sacrifices year in and year out, and never makes a dent in the sin problem. As a priest, Christ made a single sacrifice for sins, and that was it! Then he sat down right beside God and waited for his enemies to cave in. It was a perfect sacrifice by a perfect person to perfect some very imperfect people. By that single offering, he did everything that needed to be done for everyone who takes part in the purifying process.* MSG

Like the younger son, you may have found yourself in a pit of sin, addiction, despair and turmoil, but with the help of Jesus, the once and for all Passover lamb, you can get out of that pit, repent, and turn for home where you will find your heavenly father waiting on the road with arms wide open to receive you back into right standing. You have moved out of denial of every hurt, habit and hang-up and found he was not only willing to forgive, but to restore your personal temple so Holy Spirit has a secure dwelling place. With his Spirit living in you, there is a supernatural power to overcome temptation and to be assured he will always provide a way of escape from every evil that confronts you.

Isn't it amazing that these steps of recovery have been written for centuries, and yet we still stumble over the same dysfunctional behaviors and allow our individual temples to be contaminated repeatedly? They aren't a magic potion but rather guidelines which must be applied daily to our lives so we can exist as recovered, restored individuals. The debris that contaminates our personal temple, our body, must be removed and destroyed; then replaced with a renewed mind and heart. Then we will be empowered by Holy Spirit to not just move into recovery, but live daily in a recovered state.

I thank God daily for the steps! Knowing the steps isn't merely an academic exercise. You must understand what they are saving you from and what they are saving you to. Then you must apply each step to your life individually. But after applying them to your life, what is next?

CHAPTER 11

After working the steps, what?

YOU HAVE MOVED OUT of denial that you have hurts, habits and hang-ups in your life; confessed each issue; recognized you are powerless to save yourself; turned every area of your life over to God's care and control; undertaken the writing of a thorough, honest inventory of your life; become willing to forgive those who have harmed you and made amends to those you have hurt; begun to praise God for his redeeming work in your life and received Jesus as your Savior who alone can redeem you to a life of lasting inner healing and peace. But that isn't where the journey ends. You must trust the process and walk the path of recovery and restoration daily.

God assures us the restored individual temple is far better than the former one you had. Why would he enable your personal temple to be cleaned up and then allow it to be re-contaminated? Hag 2:9 reassures us it will be a place of peace.

> 'The glory of this present house will be greater than the glory of the former house,' says the Lord Almighty. 'And in this place I will grant peace,' declares the Lord Almighty. NIV

It is extremely important to *keep the steps ever before you*. Whenever you sense insecurity about your stability, face obstacles on your journey, confront temptation to act out or even become complacent in your recovery; I strongly suggest taking the steps out and reviewing them once again. Always go back to the first step of opening the doors of your life and admitting specifically what you are dealing with. Work the steps until every issue is turned over, examined and dealt with. Toss the debris out and ask Holy Spirit, who now lives in you, to renew your mind and redirect your path. I repeat Rom 12:2 for emphasis.

> *Do not conform to the pattern of this world, but be transformed by the renewing of your mind. Then you will be able to test and approve what God's will is—his good, pleasing and perfect will.* NIV

It is also critical to *stay in God's Word daily, pray daily, and keep a daily inventory by journaling and recording every issue you confront.* Remember to not only record the challenges and occasional slip ups, but also reward yourself when you successfully overcome through the power of God living in your temple.

Another critical part of your journey is to learn to *look for and listen to his direction to the avenues of escape from temptation* that God promises to provide for you. Just because you have admitted every hurt, habit and hang-up in your life; turned them all over to God's care and control; are being given the ability to deal with the acute and chronic effects of your dysfunctional behaviors and have accepted Jesus as the one who can forgive and set you free from every sin and addiction; doesn't mean there won't be temptations along the way to go back to your former way of living. In those times you can rely on the fact God promises to provide a way out of the situation if you will look and listen for it as found in I Cor 10:12–13.

> *So, if you think you are standing firm, be careful that you don't fall! No temptation has overtaken you except what is common to mankind. And God is faithful; he will not let you be tempted beyond what you can bear. But when you are tempted, he will also provide a way out so that you can endure it.* NIV

The key is to be alert to determining where the door to the way of escape is located and either don't enter to begin with, or if you have taken a step through, be sure to exit immediately. You cannot continue running with the same crowd, going to the same places and doing the same things as you did before your personal temple was restored. It has been cleared and cleaned so don't contaminate it again. Many individuals I have worked with in recovery programs assumed a short period of sobriety from their habit of choice meant it was now their responsibility to convince persons they used to run with to join them on the recovery journey. As badly as you want to reach out to them however; going back into environments with triggers and temptations to act out is not prudent and can easily lead you into relapse.

Finally, once your temple has been restored and you are living in a clean place where Holy Spirit can dwell, it is time to begin to tell others about what God has done for you. In the story described to us in Mark 5 and Luke 8 about the man named Legion who had many addictions, Jesus didn't say come and follow me, but told him to go and tell everyone about what had happened to him. His personal temple had been restored, his chains broken and he had a remarkable story to tell all over the Decapolis. Two chapters later, four thousand men plus women and children came to hear the good news of the gospel. I suspect many of them were influenced by the testimony of Legion.

In Matt 9 we find a story of a paralyzed man who was brought to Jesus in Nazareth for healing; in Mark 2 and Luke 5 a description of a man with paralysis lowered through the roof to Jesus for healing; and in John 5 the well-known story of the man who had laid by the pool at Bethesda for thirty-eight years in pain. In each instance, after healing them, Jesus told them to get up (trust me), and walk (obey me), but he also instructed them to pick up their mats. Their mat was the place where they had resided in their disease and paralysis. Jesus restored their bodies to health so Holy Spirit could reside there and then told them to carry their mat, which was their testimony, with them and tell everyone, who had healed them and what God had done for them.

These words had such a powerful effect on Peter, he used them when he healed a man who had been paralyzed for eight years. Acts 9:33–34

> There he found a man named Aeneas, who was paralyzed and had been bedridden for eight years. "Aeneas," Peter said to him, "Jesus Christ heals you. Get up and roll up your mat." Immediately, Aeneas got up. NIV

In the same way, you should use your mat to open doors of opportunity to relate your personal restoration story of how God has cleaned up your individual temple and redeemed your life from one of sin and addiction to one of wholeness and peace. I have had the pleasure of witnessing the impact of many restored persons sharing their mat with others when the time was right, in order to proclaim the message of emotional and relational healing they have received. I will share some of those with you in the next chapter.

CHAPTER 12

Examples of Restored Temples

READING ABOUT THE STEPS of restoration outlined by Hezekiah and correlating them with Paul's allegorical comparison to our bodies being temples where Holy Spirit can dwell is intriguing, but does applying those steps to our individual lives actually result in renewal and transformation? I have been so blessed to see the completion of this work in persons who many had written off as beyond recovery. Yes, there have been some who refused to work the steps; failed to move out of denial of their issues; succumbed to temptation and relapsed into their addictions. We have even witnessed some deaths from overdose and criminal behavior. But there have been far more stories of restoration and I want to encourage you by relating some of them; protecting their identity by using an initial for their name. In each of these instances the individual was able to move past the *what*, (the sin or addiction others saw) and deal with the *why* (the reason or reasons behind their acting out). In doing so they were able to identify the *root issues* causing their dysfunctional behavior and move into restored living by working the 7 steps previously outlined for you.

THE RESTORATION OF "B"

"B" was raised in a broken home by his mother and step-father. He experienced emotional and physical abuse from his step-father, and as is so typical, his mother defended her husband's behavior. "B" felt abandoned and rejected. He felt he could never measure up to the expectations of others. In order to find acceptance, he began to associate with a group of young men who were also filled with anger and rage for various reasons. He learned to defend himself physically by using his fists and eventually guns. He was always attempting to get back at his step-father by hurting others. Theft became a part of his acting out as well. In his late teen years, he was arrested and imprisoned for assault and battery after beating a man senseless.

"B" had never been to church in his life. He refused to attend the prison chapel services, but since he enjoyed reading, frequently went to the prison library where he began to delve into books about the religions of the world. Eventually he picked up a Bible and the first book he turned to was the book of Romans. Paul's words in chapters 6, 7 and 8 penetrated his heart and mind. One night in his prison cell, he experienced the presence of God's Spirit and heard him say, "Surrender your life to my care and control and I will give you true peace." There in a lonely prison cell he cried out, "I don't know who you are, but I want to be free of anger and rage and I want you as the father-figure in my life."

"B" asked the chaplain for a Bible and began to read and study it daily. Without any formal Biblical training, the word became clear to him, and he was able to surrender more and more of himself to Jesus. He had a deep hunger to not only know God, but to please him by living a restored life. When he was paroled, he found a church home and a recovery group in which he was accepted without reservation. Step by step he began to give up dysfunctional behaviors including the use of drugs, alcohol, and nicotine. He has remained sober and free of acting out in anger. He has been able to forgive his step-father without condoning his behavior. "B" picks up his mat frequently to tell others about the restoration found in his personal relationship with Jesus!

THE RESTORATION OF "J"

"J" was raised in a Christian home by parents who felt the best way to discourage dysfunctional sexual activity was to avoid discussing it. Any mention of sex was met with shame and discipline. In his teen years, "J" began to act out sexually with different girls. He never maintained a relationship and felt the way to prove himself was to conquer as many women as he could. Following high school and college, he attended seminary and became a youth pastor. He never admitted his sexual dysfunction to anyone, even the woman he married. His acting out didn't stop with his pastoral appointment. Now he was in close contact with attractive girls and that accelerated his inappropriate desires. Fortunately, he did not interact with teenage females.

Each inappropriate interaction resulted in shame and guilt. Eventually, "J" sought us out for help, however, he wanted the *what* (his acting out) to go away without identifying and dealing with the *why* (the reasons behind his behavior). When told he must admit and confess his behavior to his wife and to the church, he refused. Two more years of infidelity followed. Finally, experiencing deep inner turmoil and desperation, "J" confessed everything. He received counseling and began to attend a recovery group regularly. Instead of rejection and condemnation, he found a love he had never known from his remarkable wife and from his church family and accountability partners. When his personal temple was cleared of all the contamination, he was able to start the difficult process of rebuilding and restoring it with the help of others who had struggled with similar issues. He is now leading recovery groups himself and walking in total sexual sobriety!

THE RESTORATION OF "G"

"G" was raised in a Southern town by loving parents and siblings. He had spent most of his younger days in a neighborhood that was primarily Black. In elementary school and middle school, he experienced racial discrimination and profiling. His heart was hardened by anger and hate. As a high school athlete, he was able to take out some of his emotions on the playing field, but still had deep-seated rage within. When he was arrested for possible possession of narcotics; the White judge misassigned his case and he missed the hearing through no fault of his own. This accelerated his anger and disgust for persons he perceived disliked him due to his skin color. The charges were dismissed, but the emotional damage was done. He fostered a desire to gain revenge and harm others for what happened to him.

"G" began to smoke pot and cigarettes as well as drink alcohol heavily. His addictions worsened over time. He had grown up in church, but had not attended regularly in years. His mother however, never stopped praying for him. One night he was awakened from sleep by a dream and a voice he heard clearly saying, "G, I love you just as you are. I want you to follow me." He knew in his heart it was the voice of God. He fell to his knees and pleaded with God for forgiveness. A light was shining through the window as if to say, "All is forgiven." The contamination of his personal temple was removed, and was replaced by the Spirit of God. He agreed to begin attending church with his mother.

"G" mistakenly walked into a men's recovery program one evening, thinking it was a prayer group. He has attended regularly since that night. His testimony describes how his desire for alcohol, drugs, and nicotine was taken away the night he surrendered his life to Jesus, after hearing him call out as he did to Samuel centuries ago. Immediate deliverance from substance use, and sexual dysfunction is not common. For most, it is a process of asking God to enable one to be set free of the desire and then trusting the process of deliverance on a daily basis. For "G" however, it occurred in an instant. A moment of blind faith and submission to God's will. He now leads a recovery program for former inmates, and is an example of how an individual temple can be restored in a miraculous way.

THE RESTORATION OF "R"

"R" was raised in a home where her mother's brother lived with her mother, father and sister. From a young age, she was sexually abused by her uncle. She was made to feel it was something she desired and it was her fault. She was warned to never tell anyone or harm would come to her mother.

As she grew older, "R" developed a hatred for men in general. She became very promiscuous; never considering a lasting relationship because of her deep-seated anger and rage. She became pregnant and delivered a healthy baby girl whom her mother raised. She became involved in a same-sex relationship but found no satisfaction there either. When she attended one of our recovery group meetings, she was greeted by persons who accepted her regardless of her past. She was not judged or condemned. When the story of Mary Magdalene was read to her, she came to the realization that forgiveness and restoration was possible, even for her.

Flashbacks and horrible memories troubled her daily. A group of women prayed for her and enabled her to understand Jesus had the power to remove those tragic recollections from her mind just as he had for Mary Magdalene as described in Luke 8:2. She experienced a dramatic restoration of her mind and spirit. The flashbacks and troubling dreams miraculously stopped. She has become a witness of God's willingness to forgive, heal and restore lives. Due to her own experiences, she is uniquely able to reach out to other women who have been abused and neglected.

THE RESTORATION OF "L"

"L" was raised in a Christian home where his mother was the primary believer. His father worked late hours; was often not at home; and had extramarital relationships. The absence of a father-figure in the home impacted "L's" self-image and caused him to feel he could never do enough to measure up. He sought security by associating with young men and women who drank heavily and used drugs. After finishing high school, he moved away from home in an attempt to get a fresh start in life. Instead, he developed friendships with persons just like the ones he had left. Heavy alcohol use, cocaine addiction and sleeping with prostitutes became his daily way of life.

One night he stumbled upon a Bible he had in his closet. He read the book of John and came to the realization that God the father loved us so much he was willing to give us his only son to restore our lives and seal our redemption as the Passover lamb. He had always thought of a father as one who was absent and not dependable; but the words he read described a daddy who loved him and would never leave or abandon him. He read John 14:6 and prayed, "Jesus, I want to know your father and I want you to come and live in my heart and mind. Please forgive me and restore me." A feeling of warmth and acceptance swept over him and he knew he was different.

He moved again, but this time was determined to find a church home where he could plant roots and develop sound friendships. His desire for substances and sex went away progressively. In recovery, he became aware that his root issue was a father-wound, and as a result of that woundedness he had turned to substances and sex to attempt to fill the void in his life. He was able to receive God's restoration of his individual temple, and realized the chains that bound him were broken and he was set free to be the man God intended him to be. He now leads others in their search for similar freedom from bondage.

THE RESTORATION OF "C"

"C" was raised in a home where any discussion of sexual topics was considered taboo. He had no one with whom he could talk about his questions and desires. He was introduced to pornography by a friend and soon became obsessed with viewing images of women and acting out. He developed a false image of what sexual intimacy was intended to be and had a distorted view of the self-worth of females. His addiction continued into his high-school and college years, leading to guilt, frustration and self-condemnation.

A friend invited "C" to attend church where the message that Sunday was from the text of Rom 12:2. He realized his need for a transformation of his mind and heart. This young man experienced a release from his desire for pornography and unhealthy sex. He was amazed by the supernatural power of God to set him free and break the chains of addiction that bound him when he was prayed for by men who had experienced the same deliverance. He is now bold in his proclamation to other men about the *chain-breaker* who transformed his life. He has processed and incorporated the steps of recovery into his own life and is called to minister to other men with sexual addictions.

THE RESTORATION OF "M"

"M" was raised in a broken home by his mother. He had experienced rejection by his father from a young age. He struggled in school; had few friends; and felt he could never measure up to the standards set before him. "M" began to associate with a group of older men who introduced him to satanic worship and pagan beliefs. They encouraged him to begin to drink heavily and use drugs. Soon, he was addicted and was selling to support his habit.

He had learned martial arts in order to defend himself. A drug deal gone bad resulted in assault and battery charges when he nearly beat a man to death. He was jailed and as is often the case, the penal system did nothing to restore him from his habits, anger and rage.

When "M" was paroled, he went right back to his old friends and began to sell drugs again in order to support himself. He was at the home of the man who had introduced him to pagan worship practices when the flashing lights of a sheriff's car nearby caught his attention. Thinking they were coming for him and knowing he was in violation of his parole for being there, he ran out the back door of the home and into a forest. He had no idea where he was going as he ran through the trees and bushes. Suddenly, a bright light was shining down on him and he assumed it was a police helicopter, but he didn't hear the whir of helicopter blades. The light guided him through the forest and eventually into a clearing. Immediately, the light disappeared, and he recognized the road he was approaching. He was able to walk home, confused about the events which had transpired.

Two days later, "M" asked to meet with me to talk about what had happened. He related the story and asked me what it meant? I explained to him that the light had to be from God who was attempting to get his attention, and had guided him to safety. Why, I couldn't explain, but I told him this may be his only chance to have his life restored and changed. I asked him if he wanted to accept Jesus as the Lord and Savior of his life? He replied, "I would like to, but I can't say his name." He explained that in satanic worship the name of Jesus can never be used. I explained to him, "God has reached out to you and is offering to save you from this lifestyle of anger, violence, drugs and pagan beliefs. But you will have to call on the name of Jesus to experience salvation." He struggled for several minutes to say Jesus' name. Eventually, he was able to say, "Jesus, I believe in you and I want to give my life to your care and control." A peace and calm came over him and he was set free from his addictions. A few weeks later he was baptized.

I told him he must change his friends and stop going to the places he had been frequenting. I indicated it would not be easy, but God promises to show you the way of escape from temptation if you will listen and look for it. God saw worth in a person whom most had given up on. He will go to great lengths to get our attention and lead us to his Son, although it may not be as dramatically as it was with "M".

These are just a few of the miraculous stories of lives that have been transformed by the restoration of their personal temples through the power of God's Spirit. These persons have gotten up (trusted), walked (obeyed) but also picked up their mats which are their testimonies and are telling others about their journey of restoration and recovery.

However, once the individual temple is restored it is crucial to trust the process and continue the journey daily. As powerful as Hezekiah's 7 steps to restoration were; he couldn't maintain his own renewal and allowed deep-seated root issues to alter his course resulting in a lapse into dysfunctional behavior.

CHAPTER 13

Lapsing Into Destruction

HEZEKIAH ACHIEVED GREAT SUCCESS as king of Judah. We read in II Chron 31 and 32 that he built up their military strength and wealth. The nation accumulated great treasure and the King had it stored in large warehouses. Shortly after this, Judah was threatened by King Sennacherib and the Assyrian army (II Chron 32). Hezekiah called on the prophet Isaiah and together they prayed that God would come to their aid. God answered their prayers and the Assyrians were destroyed in dramatic fashion. Eventually, Sennacherib was killed by his own sons (II Chron 32:20–21).

Soon after, Hezekiah became terminally ill with an infection (II Chron 32:24 and Isa 38:1). He cried out to God and reminded him how he had faithfully served and obeyed him. God relented and gave Hezekiah fifteen additional years of life. However, King Hezekiah did not respond to this miracle with true thanksgiving and praise. As II Chron 32:25 says,

> But Hezekiah's heart was proud and he did not respond to the kindness shown him; therefore the Lord's wrath was on him and on Judah and Jerusalem. NIV

Other nations, including Babylon, heard about Hezekiah's success and came to visit him. In his lust for wealth, fame and power, he did what Isaiah advised him to avoid doing and showed the Babylonians all of his possessions and his military strength. As

II Chron 32:31 says, God left him to test him and know everything that was in his heart. God was displeased with Hezekiah's choice to honor himself and eventually Babylon conquered Judah and carried off all of her wealth.

So, here is the story of a man who was spiritually inclined and was led to establish recovery guidelines which would enable the temple of God to be restored. Those same guidelines carry over to us in recovery ministry today. But because he lived in denial of his deep-seated root issues of greed and a desire to be in control; he didn't follow through and trust the process to the end.

This reminds me of the rich, young ruler who came to Jesus asking what he needed to do to achieve eternal life (Matt 19:16–30, Mark 10:17–31 and Luke 18:18–30). This young man told Jesus that he had never broken even a single commandment, but Jesus saw his heart and realized, like Hezekiah, he had the root issues of control and greed which needed to be dealt with. He was told to get rid of his wealth and then submit himself to Jesus leadership by following him. Unfortunately, he couldn't give those things up and went away sad.

Apparently, Hezekiah had a lust for material possessions and for the praise of others. When we hear the word lust, our thoughts usually turn first to sexual issues. But lust is actually an unhealthy desire to have something that is not our's or is not beneficial to us. It is an attitude of the mind; a disposition of the heart. Lust is very similar to coveting. The Hebrew word for covet is *chamad* which means to have a strong desire for someone or something. It is thus a yearning to possess or a determination to have or control something. Persons usually lust because they have deep-seated root issues such as insecurity, a feeling they don't measure up, unmet expectations in their life, and a desire for temporary satisfaction rather than permanent fulfillment. The tenth commandment found in Ex 20:17 says,

> *You shall not covet your neighbor's house. You shall not covet your neighbor's wife, or his male or female servant, his ox or donkey, or anything that belongs to your neighbor.* NIV

Jesus addressed the issue of lust in his mountain-side message found in Matt 5:27–28,

> You have heard that it was said, 'You shall not commit adultery', but I say to you that everyone who [so much as] looks at a woman with lust has already committed adultery with her in his heart. Amp

Hezekiah understood all of this. He outlined steps of restoration that can still be applied to our personal temples. Yet, he never dealt with his own lust for power and things. God healed him from a deadly illness and gave him fifteen additional years of life, but instead of continuing to do the bucket work necessary to live a victorious, recovered life, he gave in to his lusts and brought devastation upon his nation. We can't put our root issues on hold or completely ignore them. They must be identified, dealt with appropriately and pursued for the rest of our lives. Hezekiah heard God's word and followed his directions for restoration, but did not apply them to his own life. James talked about this in James 1:22–25,

> Do not merely listen to the word, and so deceive yourselves. Do what it says. Anyone who listens to the word but does not do what it says is like someone who looks at his face in the mirror and, after looking at himself, goes away and immediately forgets what he looks like. But whoever looks intently into the perfect law that gives freedom, and continues in it—not forgetting what they have heard, but doing it—they will be blessed in what they do. NIV

In our society today, we have seen many Christian leaders who have forgotten what they looked like and haven't continued in the restoration process over the long haul. As unfair as it may seem, leaders are held to a higher standard of behavior. They can't develop guidelines and teach principles, but then violate them in their own personal lives. Their personal temples must remain clean and in good repair.

To stay focused and on track in keeping our individual temples restored requires:

1. Doing the bucket work of moving out of denial of our issues and turning our lives and wills over to God's care and control

2. Trusting the process of restoration daily

3. Admitting every hurt, habit and hang-up in our lives

4. Acknowledging we are powerless to save ourselves and are in need of a Savior whose name is Jesus

5. Working the steps of restoration frequently and when we fall, go back to Step one

6. Asking for forgiveness and making amends when needed

7. Staying in the Word, in prayer and in fellowship with others of like mind

When we do these things, we are much better equipped to stay the course and avoid lapses in our behavior. Allowing our personal temple to be restored is all about choice. Will we choose to do it the world's way, or will we choose to allow God to initiate and continue the renewal process? Choosing to work the steps daily is a recipe for inner healing and peace. We may not be perfect temples, but restored enough that God can use us to pick up our mats, and begin to explain to others what the process of restoration is all about!

CHAPTER 14

Restoration Is a Choice

GOD DOESN'T FORCE US to choose him or his way of life. From the very beginning with Adam and Eve, he has allowed us the freedom to choose his way or the world's way; right or wrong; life or death. His way is choosing to give rather than get; serve rather than be served; forgive in order to be forgiven; and die to self rather than live for the flesh.

The process of restoration involves a choice we must make to allow him to renew our mind and heart in order for Holy Spirit to inhabit our individual temple. The entire process involves faith and trust. It requires being rather than attempting to do more and more to gain his acceptance. The Word makes it clear in Rom 7:6 and Eph 2:8–9.

> *But now, by dying to what once bound us, we have been released from the law so that we serve in the new way of the Spirit, and not in the old way of the written code.* NIV

> *For it is by grace you have been saved, through faith—and this is not from yourselves, it is the gift of God—not by works, so that no one can boast.* NIV

Perhaps you are thinking, what do the ancient guidelines established by Hezekiah have to do with my current struggles to survive? Appropriating those steps to your life requires a choice. The apostle Paul wrote in Rom 7 about how difficult this choice was for even him to make. He said he was so caught up in the world's way of doing things that he often chose to do what he actually didn't want to do. He understood what God's law said and meant, but he couldn't fulfill it because his temple was in disrepair due to sinful desires and acts. He described to the Romans, the only path of rescue and restoration was in a personal relationship with Jesus Christ, the Passover lamb, *Hezekiah's seventh step.*

How can right choices positively affect the reconstruction of your temple? You can see your mind conformed to his will. You can experience freedom from the chains of addiction that bind you. You can find yourself doing things that honor God and the Kingdom. You can be enabled to choose the right persons to associate with and better places to frequent. You can find help along the way to keep you focused and on task to maintain sobriety from whatever your substance of choice is. You can be made aware of the path of escape from the temptation to make poor choices. You can discover opportunities to share your journey with others.

When you make one good choice, it will lead to other good choices which then become a part of the fabric of your life. We are the sum total of our life choices, so why not make them restorative decisions rather than destructive ones? There will be many who will scoff at you for even considering such a path in life. They may even despise you for it. But remember, they are steps to transformative healing and true inner peace. Jesus talked about this in his prayer for unity found in John 17:14–21.

> *"I have given them your word and the world has hated them, for they are not of the world any more that I am of the world. My prayer is not that you take them out of the world but that you protect them from the evil one. They are not of the world, even as I am not of it. Sanctify them by the truth; your word is the truth. As you sent me into the world, I have sent them into the world. For them I sanctify myself, that they too may be truly sanctified. My prayer is not for them alone. I pray also for those who will believe in me through their message, that all of them may be one, Father, just as you are in me and I am in you. May they also be in us so that the world may believe that you have sent me."* NIV

Choosing to understand and work the steps of restoration allows you to follow a path of recovery; leading to a life-journey of inner healing toward a destination of lasting peace and joy. Don't attempt to walk this path alone. Become a part of that three-stranded cord to gain the strength you need to complete the trip successfully. Restoration is a journey toward wholeness which will not be completed until we see Jesus, face to face!

I will close with the following points of emphasis:

- The primary purpose of reconstruction of your personal temple is to create a place where Holy Spirit can dwell.

- When we need and desire restoration of our lives, the blueprint for success comes with specific instructions and guidelines not haphazard recommendations.

- Our personal temple can be desecrated by making poor choices, sometimes even after we have made an initial wise choice.

- The debris contaminating our individual temple must be identified, removed, destroyed and then replaced with a renewed mind and heart.

- Our temple can be damaged as much by disuse as by external factors.

- Don't focus as much on the *what* of your life as on the *why*.

- It isn't the felonies of life that desecrate our personal temples but rather the misdemeanors.

- To continue on the journey of a restored life you must avoid denial of your issues, persist in faith that God cares about you and has a plan to heal and renew you and trust the process of restoration every day going forward. It is a lifelong journey with eternal benefits!

> Rev 3:20: *"Look! I have been standing at the door, and I am constantly knocking. If anyone hears me calling him and opens the door, I will come in and fellowship with him and he with me.* NIV

Restoring Your Temple

My temple was filled with sin, its doors were closed up tight.

I had to move out of denial and bring everything into the light.

It took a touch of the Master to clean me up and make things right.

Restore my temple Lord, make my mind and heart brand new.

Restore my temple Lord, it can only be done by you!

Bibliography

Purkiser, W. T., ed. *Exploring the Old Testament*. Kansas City, MO: Beacon Hill Press.

Gromacki, R. G. *New Testament Survey*. Grand Rapids, MI: Baker Book House.

www.ingramcontent.com/pod-product-compliance
Lightning Source LLC
LaVergne TN
LVHW021614080426
835510LV00019B/2575